KU-646-416

How big is the ocean?

The ocean is truly ENORMOUS! It covers more than twice as much of the Earth as land does. In fact, it's made up of four oceans – the Pacific, the Atlantic, the Indian and the Arctic. Although these all have different names, they flow into each other to make one huge world ocean.

Don't go for a swim in the Arctic Ocean. It's the coldest of the oceans, and for most of the year it's covered in ice.

The Sea Is Salty

and other questions
about the oceans

Anita Ganeri

KINGFISHER

Published 2011 by Kingfisher
an imprint of Macmillan Children's Books
a division of Macmillan Publishers Limited
20 New Wharf Road, London N1 9RR
Basingstoke and Oxford
Associated companies throughout the world
www.panmacmillan.com

First published 1995 by Kingfisher

Consultants: Michael Chinery, Keith Lye

ISBN 978-0-7534-3120-7
Copyright © Macmillan Children's Books 2011

All rights reserved. No part of this publication may be
reproduced, stored in or introduced into a retrieval system
or transmitted in any form or by any means (electronic,
mechanical, photocopying, recording or otherwise), without
the prior permission of the publisher. Any person who does
any unauthorized act in relation to this publication may be
liable to criminal prosecution and civil claims for damages.

9 8 7 6 5 4 3 2
2TR/0613/WKT/UNTD/128MA

A CIP catalogue record for this book is available from
the British Library.

Printed in China

This book is sold subject to the condition that it shall not,
by way of trade or otherwise, be lent, resold, hired out, or
otherwise circulated without the publisher's prior consent in
any form of binding or cover other than that in which it is
published and without a similar condition including this
condition being imposed on the subsequent purchaser.

Illustrations: Chris Forsey 4–5, 6–7, 14–15, 20––21, 28–29,
30–31; Ruby Green cover; Nick Harris (Virgil Pomfret
Agency) 8–9; Tony Kenyon (BL Kearley) all cartoons;
Nicki Palin 10–11, 18–19; Maurice Pledger (Bernard
Thornton) 16–17, 24–25; Bryan Poole 12–13, 22–23, 26–27.

CONTENTS

Which is the biggest ocean?

These drops of water show the oceans in order of size.

The Pacific is by far the biggest ocean in the world. It's larger than the other three oceans put together, and it's also much deeper. If you look at a globe, you'll see that the Pacific reaches halfway around the world.

What's the difference between a sea and an ocean?

People often use the words sea and ocean to mean the same thing. That's fine, but to a scientist, seas are just part of an ocean – the parts that are nearest to land. The Caribbean Sea is between Central America and the Caribbean islands, for example.

Pacific

Atlantic

Indian

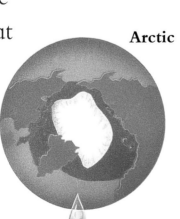

Arctic

Why is the sea salty?

Seawater tastes salty because it has salt in it! The salt is the same as the stuff people sprinkle on food. Most of it comes from rocks on the land. Rain washes the salt into rivers which carry it to the sea.

Most of the Earth's water is salty. Only a tiny part is fresh water that we can drink.

Some of the sea salt we use comes from hot places, such as India. People build low walls to trap the seawater when the tide comes in. When the Sun dries up the water, the salt is left behind.

Is the Red Sea really red?

Some beaches around the Black Sea are covered with rich, dark mud. People slap it all over themselves – it's meant to be good for the skin.

Parts of the Red Sea look red. In summer millions of tiny red plants called algae grow in the water. Don't worry, you won't turn pink if you swim there!

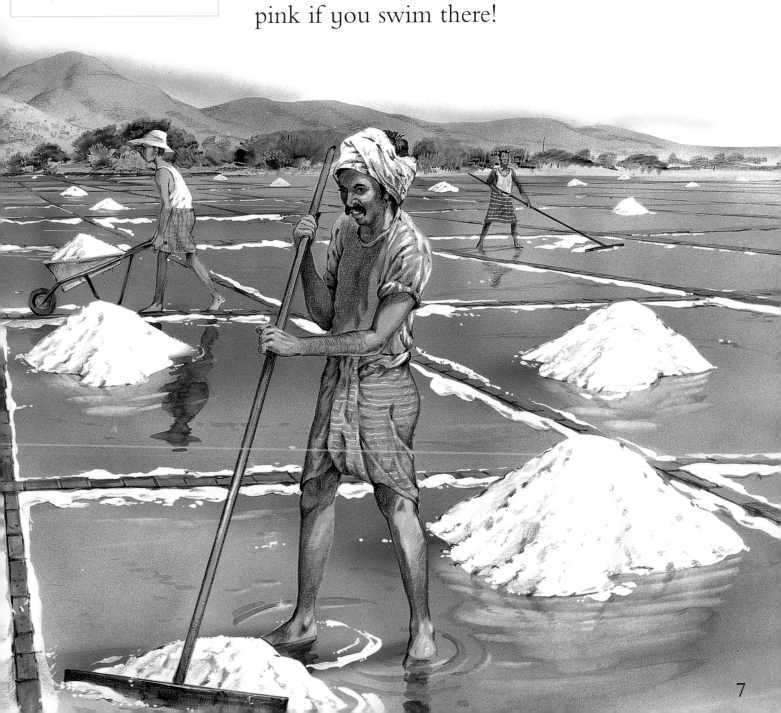

What did sailors fear the most?

 In olden days, sailors had to put up with bad food, fearful storms… and pirate attacks! Pirates roamed the high seas, on the look out for merchant ships loaded with fine goods and treasure. When the pirates found a ship they boarded it, attacked the crew, and carried off all the valuable goodies.

Blackbeard was one of the nastiest pirates. To look extra fierce, he used to thread rope through his beard and then set it on fire!

Real pirates didn't actually make people walk the plank. But the pirates you read about in stories often do!

There weren't many women pirates. Anne Bonny and Mary Read are two of the most famous. They disguised themselves as men.

Who first sailed around the world?

In 1519, a fleet of five ships set off from Spain to sail around the world. Their captain, Ferdinand Magellan, was killed on the way. Just one ship and 18 men completed the journey. It had taken three years.

Times were tough for Magellan's men. When their food ran out, they had to eat grilled leather.

What is sand made of?

Not all sand is yellow. Some beaches have black, pinky-white, or even green sand.

Look closely at a handful of sand, and you'll see that it's made of tiny chips of rock and seashell. The bits of rock come from cliffs that have been broken up by the rain and sea. The shells are washed in by the tide and crushed by the pounding waves.

Hang seaweed outside and it might forecast the weather! If it swells up, rain is on the way. If it dries out, then the Sun will shine.

Wreckers were people who shone lights to trick ships into crashing on the rocks. Then they stole all the valuable things on board, and hid them in caves.

How are caves made?

As waves hurl sand and rocks against a cliff, it is slowly worn away. The waves scoop out a small hollow, then a deep hole. After a very long time, the hole is worn into a dark, damp and dripping cave.

You can often find empty seashells washed up on the beach. Their owners have probably been eaten!

A tropical beach may look deserted, but dozens of different plants and animals make their homes there.

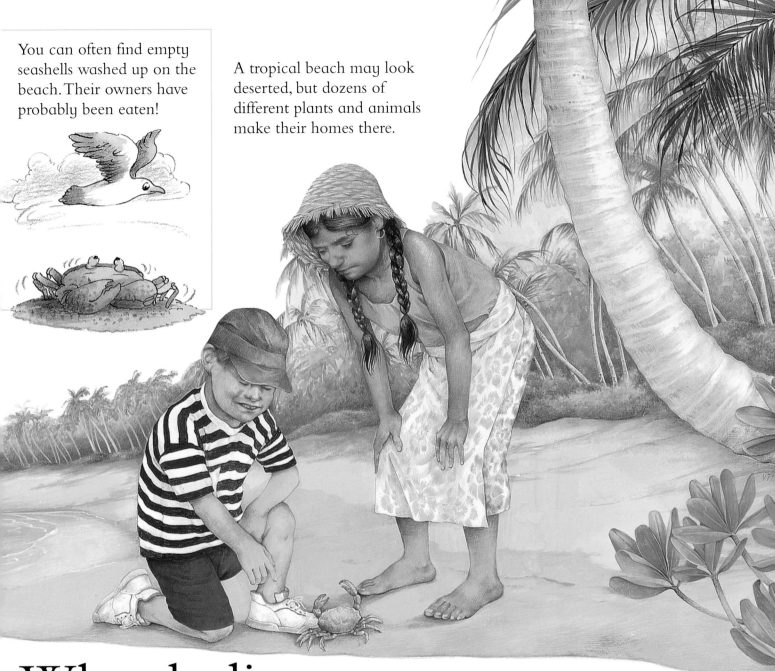

Why do limpets cling to rocks?

Like other animals on the seashore, limpets have a tough life. As the tide comes in, they are battered by the waves. As the tide goes out, they are tugged and pulled about by the swirling water. The poor limpets have to cling tightly to the rocks so that they aren't swept out to sea!

Which fish has headlights?

It's so dark at the bottom of the ocean that some fish make their own light. The angler fish has a long fin dangling in front of its face. At the end of the fin is a blob which glows. Small fish are drawn towards the glowing light, only to disappear into the angler fish's big, gaping mouth.

Angler fish

How deep is the ocean?

Away from the shore, the ocean plunges to about 4 kilometres in most places. That's deep enough to swallow Ben Nevis, Britain's tallest mountain, three times!

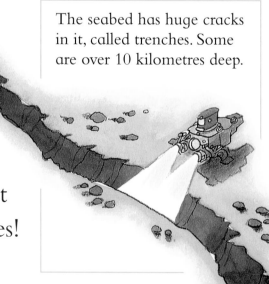

The seabed has huge cracks in it, called trenches. Some are over 10 kilometres deep.

12

What makes chimneys under the sea?

Gulper eel

Fountains of boiling hot water gush out of holes in some parts of the seabed. Tiny grains sink down out of the hot water and build into weird-looking chimney stacks around the holes.

Many deep-sea fish are real ugly mugs. It's just as well it's so dark down there!

Giant red-and-white worms as long as buses live around the chimneys.

Dragonfish

What's it like at the bottom of the sea?

You might think that the bottom of the sea is smooth and flat, but it isn't – at least not everywhere. There are mountains and valleys, hills and plains, just as there are on land.

In 1963, a volcano erupted under the sea near Iceland. Hot, runny rock bubbled up to the surface of the water, and hardened. It made a completely new island, which was named Surtsey.

Along the shore, the land slopes gently into the sea. This slope is called the continental shelf.

Flat plains cover half of the sea floor. They are called abyssal plains.

The Mid-Atlantic Ridge is a long line of underwater mountains in the Atlantic Ocean.

Are there mountains under the sea?

There are earthquakes under the sea, just as there are on land. In fact, there are over a million seaquakes a year! But most of them happen so deep down that we can't feel them.

Yes, lots – and they are all volcanoes! Someone has counted about 10,000 of them, but there may be double this number. The proper name for them is sea mounts. Some are so high that they stick out of the water and make islands.

A trench is a deep valley in the seabed.

A sea mount is an underwater volcano. There's a sea mount erupting somewhere as you read this!

How do fish breathe under water?

Not all sea creatures can breathe under water. Sea cows, seals and dolphins breathe air, so they have to keep coming to the surface.

Fish have to breathe to stay alive, just as you do. But while you breathe oxygen from the air, fish take it from water. As they swim, fish gulp in water and push it out through slits called gills on their heads. Oxygen passes from the water into the fish's blood inside their gills.

Gill cover

How do fish swim?

Fish swim by using their muscles to ripple their bodies along. Wiggling their tails from side to side gives them extra push. They use their other fins to balance and change direction.

Which bird flies under water?

Penguins can't fly through the air because their wings are too short and stumpy. They are much more at home in the ocean, where they use their wings as flippers.

Which animal is jet-propelled?

Seahorses are not strong swimmers. They hang on to seaweed to avoid being swept away.

Squid don't have flippers or a tail, but they're still fast movers. They suck water into their bodies, then squirt it out so powerfully that their bodies shoot backwards.

Squid have ten tentacles – that's two more than their relative, the octopus.

Which animal loves to play?

Dolphins are playful and trusting. Some are so friendly they will let you swim with them. Dolphins have even rescued drowning people, using their noses to nudge them to shore.

How do whales and dolphins use sound to see?

Whales and dolphins use ears, not eyes, to find their way about. As they swim they make clicking noises, which travel through the water. When the clicks hit something solid, an echo bounces back – just like a ball bouncing off a wall. The echo tells the animal what lies ahead.

Dolphins have up to 200 sharp, pointed teeth for holding on to slippery fish. Imagine brushing those every night!

Narwhals are a kind of whale with a very long tusk. Sailors used to sell narwhal tusks, pretending they were the horns of unicorns!

Which sea animals sing like birds?

White beluga whales are nicknamed 'sea canaries' because they cheep and chirrup like birds. They can also moo like cows, chime like bells, or press their lips together in a loud smack!

What makes waves roll?

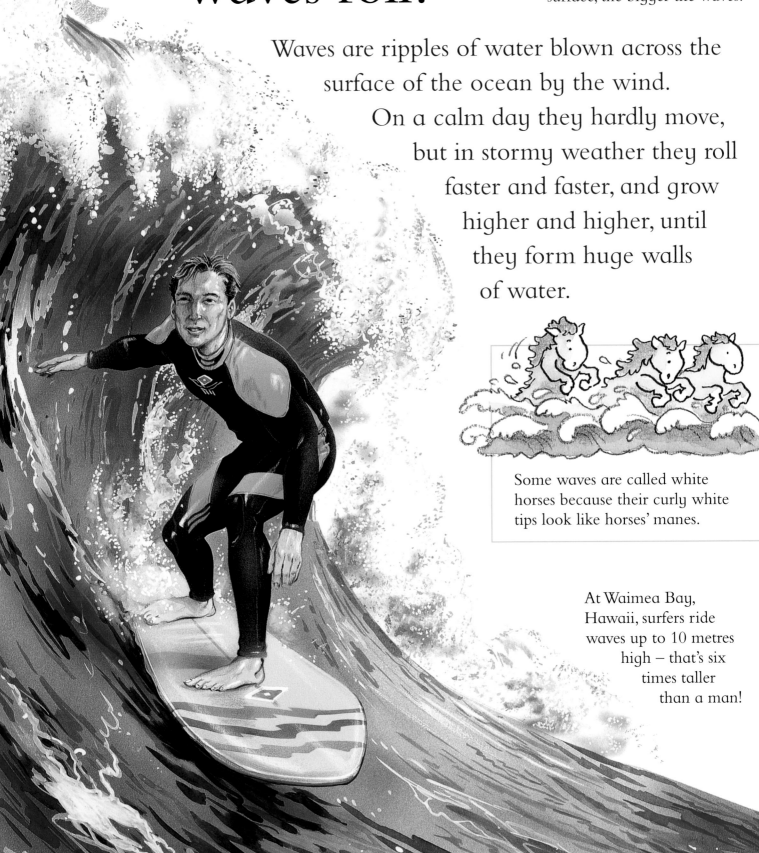

You can make your own waves in a bowl of water. The harder you blow across the surface, the bigger the waves.

Waves are ripples of water blown across the surface of the ocean by the wind. On a calm day they hardly move, but in stormy weather they roll faster and faster, and grow higher and higher, until they form huge walls of water.

Some waves are called white horses because their curly white tips look like horses' manes.

At Waimea Bay, Hawaii, surfers ride waves up to 10 metres high – that's six times taller than a man!

Are there rivers in the ocean?

Palm trees will grow in a chilly place like Scotland because warm currents flow along the west coast, bringing water from much hotter parts of the world.

The ocean has great bands of water called currents which flow like rivers. They travel faster than the water around them, moving from one part of the world to another.

Ocean currents can carry a message in a bottle for you. But don't hold your breath. One floated for 73 years before it was washed up!

Why do sailors watch the tide?

In Canada's Bay of Fundy, the water at high tide is about 15 metres deeper than at low tide – that's the height of a five-storey house!

Twice a day the sea comes high up the beach, and then goes back again. At high tide the water is deep, and sailing boats can sail in and out of the harbour. But at low tide, the water is so shallow that sailors are either stuck on the shore or out at sea!

Where do angels, clowns and parrots live?

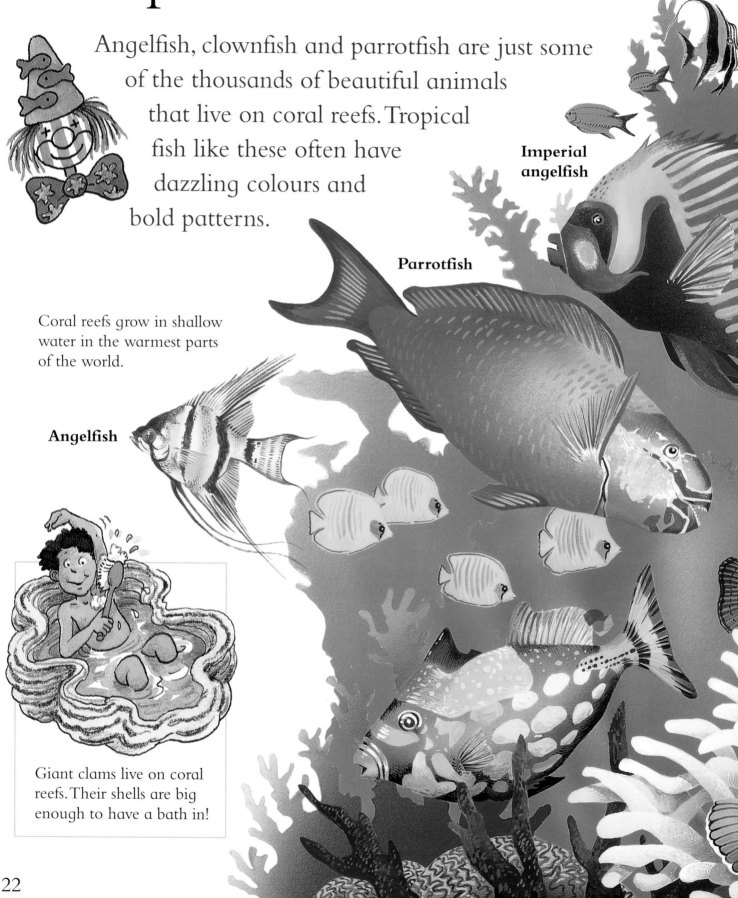

Angelfish, clownfish and parrotfish are just some of the thousands of beautiful animals that live on coral reefs. Tropical fish like these often have dazzling colours and bold patterns.

Imperial angelfish

Parrotfish

Coral reefs grow in shallow water in the warmest parts of the world.

Angelfish

Giant clams live on coral reefs. Their shells are big enough to have a bath in!

What is a coral reef?

A coral reef is like a beautiful underwater hedge. It looks stony and dead – but it is really alive! Coral is made up of millions of tiny animals, which leave their hard skeletons behind when they die. Each new layer piles on to the old, slowly building the coral rock.

Corals come in all sorts of shapes – antlers, plates, mushrooms, feathers, daisies and even brains!

Where is the biggest reef?

The world's biggest coral reef lies in the warm shallow seas off the northeast coast of Australia. It's called the Great Barrier Reef, and it stretches for more than 2,000 kilometres. It's so huge that it can be seen by astronauts up in space.

Clown fish

23

Which is the biggest fish?

The dwarf goby is the smallest fish in the ocean.

The whale shark is the world's biggest fish. It's gigantic – as long as eight scuba divers lying head to toe, and as heavy as six large elephants.

The oar fish is the longest fish in the ocean – as long as four canoes placed end to end.

Oar fish

The biggest sea plant is the giant kelp sea-weed. A single strand can grow nearly as long as a football pitch!

Sailfish

Which is the fastest fish?

The sailfish can race along under water at over 100 kilometres an hour – as fast as a car. It tucks its fins in tightly, and its pointed nose cuts through the water like a knife.

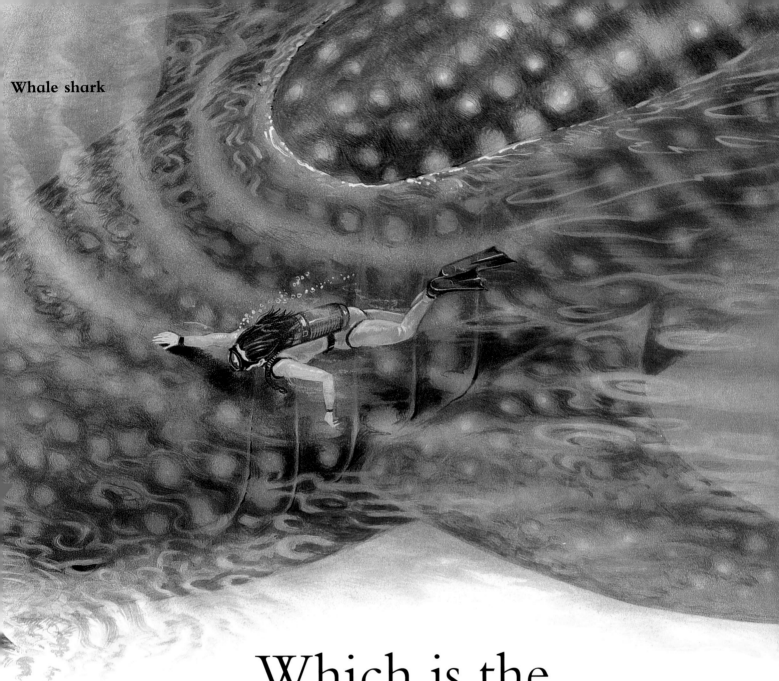

Whale shark

Which is the biggest crab?

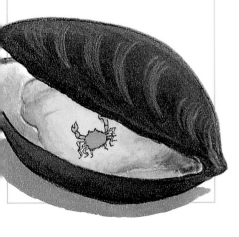

The pea-sized pea crab is the smallest crab of all. It lives inside oyster and mussel shells.

Japan's giant spider crab measures nearly 4 metres from the tip of one claw to the tip of the other. It could open its arms wide enough to hug a hippopotamus!

Which fish hunts with a hammer?

The hammerhead shark has a huge head shaped like a hammer. But this tool is for hunting, not banging in nails. The shark's eyes and nostrils are at each end of the hammer. As the shark swims, it swings its head from side to side, searching for a meal.

Which is the most shocking fish?

The Portuguese man-of-war catches its tea in its long, stinging tentacles.

Some fish give off electric shocks to protect themselves or to stun animals they want to eat. The most shocking ocean fish is the torpedo ray. If you could switch it on, it would light up a light bulb!

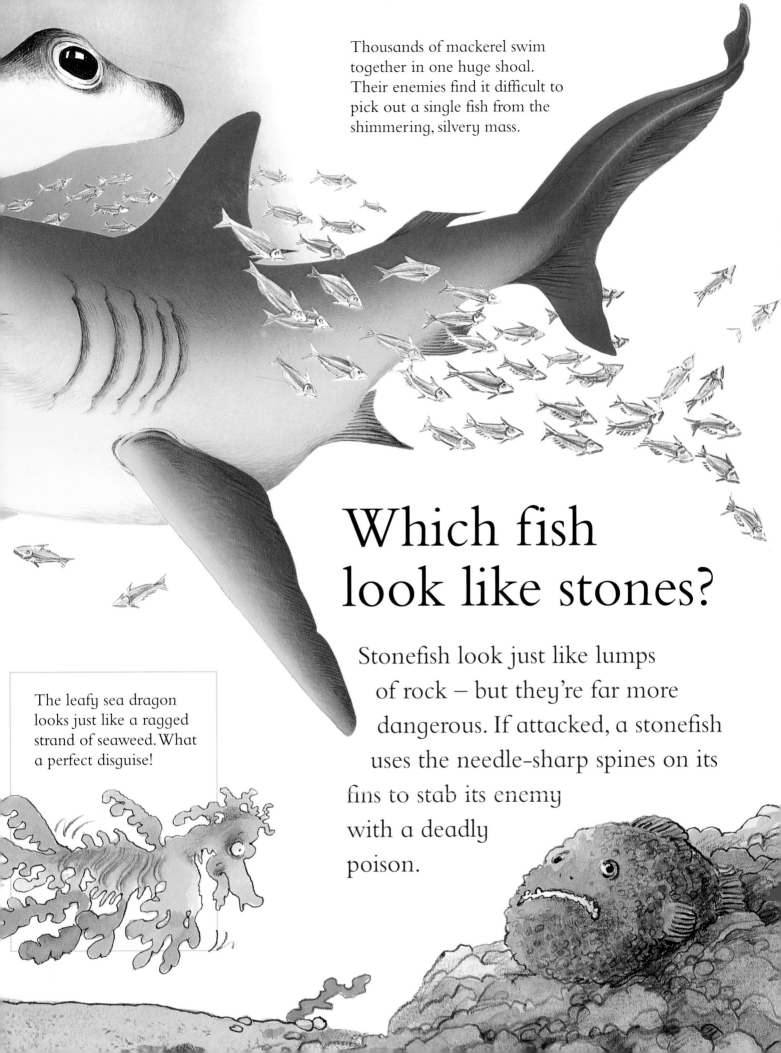

Thousands of mackerel swim
together in one huge shoal.
Their enemies find it difficult to
pick out a single fish from the
shimmering, silvery mass.

Which fish
look like stones?

Stonefish look just like lumps
of rock – but they're far more
dangerous. If attacked, a stonefish
uses the needle-sharp spines on its
fins to stab its enemy
with a deadly
poison.

The leafy sea dragon
looks just like a ragged
strand of seaweed. What
a perfect disguise!

How deep do submarines dive?

Few submarines can dive much lower than 200 metres below the surface of the ocean. That's about 100 times deeper than an Olympic swimming pool.

What dives deepest?

Divers use smaller craft called submersibles to explore deep water and to look for wrecks and sunken treasure. The *Titanic* was an enormous ocean liner which sank around 100 years ago. Divers discovered the wreck, 3,781 metres down in 1985. They were able to reach it in a submersible called *Alvin*.

The *Titanic* was launched in 1912. On its very first voyage, it hit an iceberg and sank in the Atlantic Ocean.

Which was the deepest dive ever?

In 1960 two men dived nearly 11 kilometres into the Marianas Trench in the Pacific Ocean. They were inside one of the first submersibles, an incredibly strong craft called *Trieste*. The submersible took about 5 hours to reach the bottom.

Divers wear special suits of armour in deep water. This one is called *Spider*. It's like a one-person submarine!

In the deepest parts of the ocean, the water presses down so hard that to be there would be like having ten elephants sitting on top of you!

Who fishes with fire?

On an island in the Pacific Ocean, people fish in the darkness of night. They set fire to the branches of coconut trees, and then hang them over the side of their boats. The fish swim towards the firelight – only to be caught by the islanders' sharp spears.

Seaweed is rich in goodness, so farmers spread it on their land to improve the soil. It is also used to thicken ice-cream and toothpaste.

Are there farms under the sea?

Yes, but there aren't any farmers, cows or sheep! Some kinds of fish and shellfish are raised in large cages out at sea. The fish are so well fed that they grow much more quickly than they would do in the wild.

People all over the world have different legends that tell how the world was created. Some say that it was made inside a giant clam shell. It must have been some shell!

Are there jewels in the sea?

The biggest pearl ever found was as large as your head. Imagine wearing it around your neck!

In warm tropical water, pearls may grow inside the shells of oysters and clams. The pearls are such rare finds that they are very valuable. People risk their lives diving down for them.

Index